WITHDRAWN

The Ancient ROMANS

Revised and Updated

JANE SHUTER

Heinemann Library
Chicago, Illinois

3 1267 13982 5036

© 2000, 2007 Heinemann Library
a division of Reed Elsevier Inc.
Chicago, Illinois

Customer Service 888-454-2279
Visit our website at www.heinemannraintree.com

All rights reserved. No part of this publication may be reproduced or transmitted in any form or by any means, electronic or mechanical, including photocopying, recording, taping, or any information storage and retrieval system, without permission in writing from the publisher.

Designed by Richard Parker and Q2A Solutions
Printed in China by WKT Company Ltd

11 10 09 08 07
10 9 8 7 6 5 4 3 2 1

New edition ISBNs: 13 digit ISBNs
1-403-48812-6 (hardback)   978-1-403-48812-1 (hardback)
1-403-48819-3 (paperback)   978-1-403-48819-0 (paperback)

The Library of Congress has cataloged the first edition as follows:
Shuter, Jane.
        The ancient Romans / Jane Shuter.
        p.   cm. -- (History opens windows)
        Includes bibliograhical references and index.
        Summary: An introduction to the various elements of ancient Roman
    civilization, including gods and goddesses, clothing, food, town and
    country life, government, and the army.
        ISBN 1-57572-591-6 (lib. bdg.). --ISBN 1-57572-592-4 (pbk.)
        1. Rome--Civilization--Juvenile literature.   [1. Rome--
    Civilization.].   I. Title. II. Series.
    DG78.S48   1997
    937--dc21   97-15072
                                                 CIP
                                                 AC

Acknowledgments
The author and publishers are grateful to the following for permission to reproduce copyright material:
British Museum, p. **6, 16, 20** (left); C. M. Dixon, p. **8, 18**; Veralanium Museum, p. **10**; Ancient Art & Architecture Collection Ltd./Ronald Sheridan, p. **12, 22, 25**; Bridgeman Art Library/Giraudon, p. **14**; British Library, p. **20** (right); Scala Photo Library, Italy, p. **24**; Hamlyn Group Picture Library, p. **26**; Rheinischen Landesmuseums, Trier, Germany, p. **28**.

Cover photograph reproduced with permission of The Art Archive / Archeological Museum Cividale Friuli / Dagli Orti.

Every effort has been made to contact copyright holders of any material reproduced in this book. Any omissions will be rectified in subsequent printings if notice is given to the publisher.

Contents

Some words are shown in bold, **like this**.
You can find out what they mean by looking in the glossary.

Introduction

The Roman Empire grew outward from Rome, Italy. This map shows the empire at its biggest, in about AD 100.

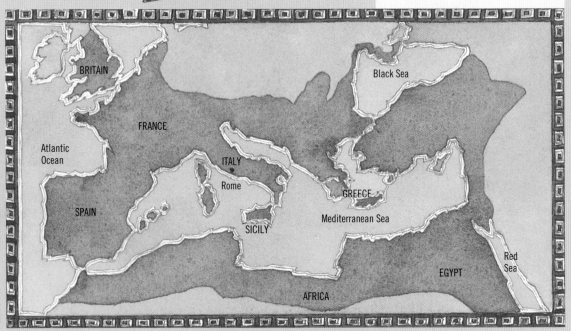

BRITAIN

Black Sea

FRANCE

Atlantic Ocean

ITALY

Rome

GREECE

Mediterranean Sea

SPAIN

SICILY

Red Sea

EGYPT

AFRICA

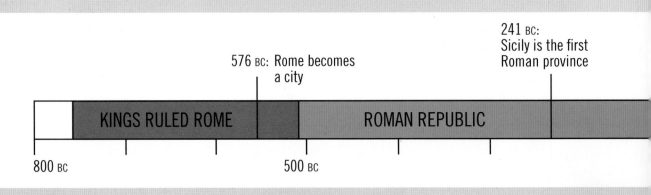

576 BC: Rome becomes a city

241 BC: Sicily is the first Roman province

KINGS RULED ROME

ROMAN REPUBLIC

800 BC

500 BC

The Romans captured and ruled many places between about 500 BC and AD 476. The center of their huge **empire** was Rome, Italy.

By about 265 BC, Rome controlled most of Italy. It kept growing. As Rome grew stronger, some countries did not want to fight. They were happy to become part of Rome. They wanted the Roman army to protect them. Each new country became a **province** of Rome, run by a Roman governor. In return for Roman protection, the provinces paid **taxes** to Rome and obeyed Roman laws.

The Roman Empire kept spreading until it got too big and it could not keep everyone safe. Slowly, it lost its provinces and its power.

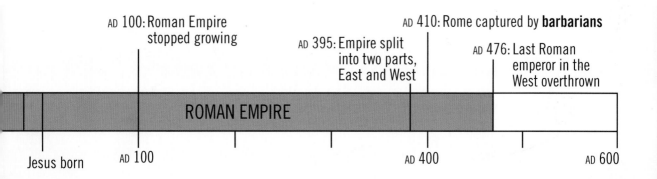

AD 100: Roman Empire stopped growing

AD 410: Rome captured by **barbarians**

AD 395: Empire split into two parts, East and West

AD 476: Last Roman emperor in the West overthrown

ROMAN EMPIRE

Jesus born

AD 100

AD 400

AD 600

How Rome Was Ruled

When Rome was a small part of Italy, it was ruled by kings. This period lasted about 200 years. But in 509 BC, the Romans threw out their king. They made Rome into a **republic**.

The Roman Republic was governed by wealthy and important Roman men called **patricians**. These men were part of the **Senate**. The Senate gave advice to two ruling **consuls**, who changed each year. All men, patricians and **plebeians**, chose the consuls. The plebeians were the ordinary people. They were supposed to have a say in how things were run. Some of the time they had more say than other times.

When they took over another country, the Romans made new coins to celebrate. These coins celebrate the capture of Egypt and Armenia.

The Roman Republic grew. The Senate took more and more power and land. The difference between wealthy and poor people grew. Patricians, plebeians, governors of **provinces**, and members of the army all scrambled for power. It was hard to govern when these people did not work together.

The Romans needed a strong leader to unite everyone. Julius Caesar was an army general who tried to unite the republic. However, he was murdered in 44 BC. Finally, the strongest of the consuls, Augustus, took over the powers of the Senate. He was the first emperor, a type of king.

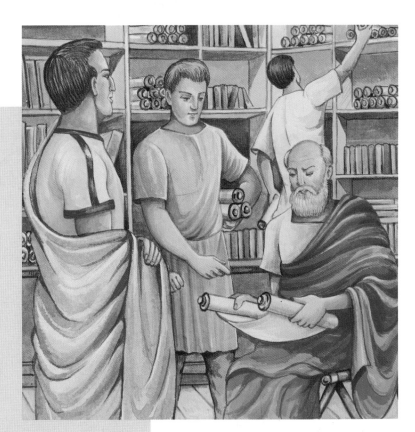

A big **empire** needed a lot of record-keeping. These officials wrote information down on paper scrolls and wax tablets. You can see the scrolls and tablets stacked on the shelves.

The Army

The Roman army was an important reason why the **empire** grew so large. At first, every Roman man had to fight. Wealthy men fought on horseback, common men fought on foot.

As the empire grew, fighting became a full-time, paid job. Roman soldiers were well trained, well organized, and well equipped. Men from all over the empire joined the army. A soldier joined the army for 15 to 20 years. At the end of this time, he was given land to farm or money to buy land.

Roman soldiers had to build things as well as fight. They had to make forts and roads and bridges to cross rivers.

A Common Roman Soldier
and his Equipment

A Roman soldier's
gear weighed about
75 pounds (35
kilograms).

Body armor
was made up of
separate pieces,
not one stiff
piece. This made
it easier for the
soldier to move.

Soldiers
held shields
over their
heads when
attacking
a wall.

Each soldier
carried two poles.
They were used
to build a fence
when the army
made a camp.

Nails were placed on the bottom of
soldiers' sandals. This helped them
get a good grip on muddy ground.

Builders and Engineers

The Romans needed good roads. The army had to move quickly. Orders from Rome had to be taken to all the **provinces**. So Roman **engineers** built a network of roads all across the **empire**.

Engineers used their skills to design huge buildings and long bridges. They also designed **aqueducts** to carry clean water to towns and cities. Many of these things were so well built that they are still standing today.

The Pont du Gard aqueduct today. It carried water to the Roman town of Nîmes. The arches give strong support to the channel that carried the water.

Building a Road

The first step was to decide where the road should go. Engineers measured from one high point to another, making the roads as straight as they could.

The builders then dug a trench. The road was built up in the trench in layers. First there was a layer of big stones. Next came a layer of gravel. This leveled off any bumps made by the big stones. Then came a layer of sand and cement.

The top layer was made of big, flat stones fitted tightly together and packed down hard. Roads were slightly higher in the middle than at the sides so water could drain off.

Gods and Goddesses

The Romans believed in many gods and goddesses, who could come to Earth and change anyone's life. So it was important to keep the gods happy. The Romans built large **temples** to their gods, such as Jupiter, who were worshiped throughout the **empire**. Smaller temples were built to less important gods. When Romans became Christians, they had to give up all their other gods.

Most people had a shrine in their homes. They prayed to the lares, or household gods, at this shrine. They also prayed to their dead relatives.

If a new province had different gods, the Romans accepted them. When the Romans conquered Greece, they found that the Greek gods were like their own. For example, the Greek god Zeus was like the Roman god Jupiter, and the Greek goddess Hera was like the Roman goddess Juno.

A small temple to the goddess Minerva. Temples were built in this style all over the empire.

Town Life

A butcher's shop. The butcher is cutting meat. Cut pieces hang from hooks and there is a bowl to throw the bones and fat into.

Roman towns and cities were busy places. The biggest and most important city in the **empire** was Rome. But many smaller towns all over the empire had all the things the people needed.

A Roman town needed a forum. This was a large central square with shops and temples. People met here to do business or talk about politics. A town needed at least one public bath house, a theater, and many houses, shops, and workshops.

A small Roman town. People came to it from all around to buy and sell things in the market.

Country Life

Most Romans lived and worked in the countryside. They grew crops to feed the **empire**. People in different parts of the empire grew different crops, depending on the soil and the weather. In hot parts they grew grapes and olives. In cold parts they grew turnips and apples. Most farmers grew wheat for flour.

Some people worked for themselves on small farms. They grew enough food to feed their families, with maybe a little left over to sell at the local market. Other people worked on large farms on lands that belonged to rich **patricians**.

This statue of a farmer plowing with oxen was found in Britain. Oxen were used on farms all over the empire.

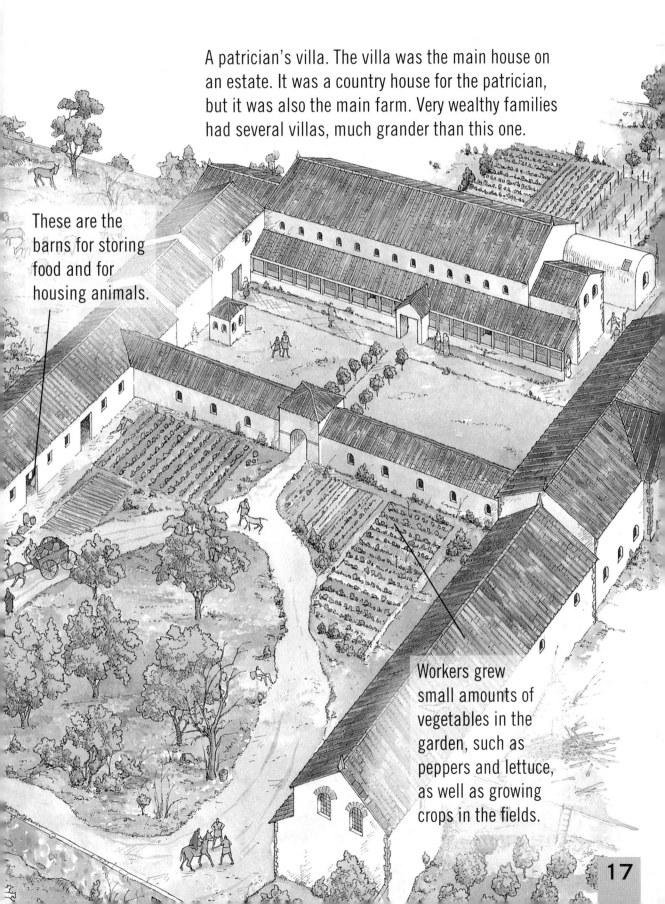

A patrician's villa. The villa was the main house on an estate. It was a country house for the patrician, but it was also the main farm. Very wealthy families had several villas, much grander than this one.

These are the barns for storing food and for housing animals.

Workers grew small amounts of vegetables in the garden, such as peppers and lettuce, as well as growing crops in the fields.

Family Life

This carving from Rome shows a mother bathing her baby with the help of a slave.

The Romans had very clear ideas about how families should be run. The paterfamilias, or father, was the head of the family. Everyone had to obey him, even his grown-up children. Men were supposed to work and do business outside the home. Women were supposed to run the home and care for the children.

All but the poorest families had **slaves** to work for them. Slaves were part of the family. They were mostly people who had been captured in battle. Some were treated well, others were not. Slaves could buy their freedom if they could save enough money.

A Wealthy Family's Home

The daughter and her friends have a late breakfast. Her mother gives orders to the cook.

Slaves clean the bedroom, while the son's wife dresses. Her baby is asleep in the cradle.

The father and his son are in the study.

Slaves keep the fire going for the hypocaust, or heating system.

The floor is raised on pillars. Warm air goes under the floor and rises to heat the house.

A slave takes a visitor to see the father.

Children

Children started school at the age of seven. Most boys went to school. Girls of wealthy families went to school and learned to run a home. Girls of poor families learned to spin, weave, cook, and clean. At school, children learned to read and write Latin and Greek and do math. Boys spent more time at school than girls.

When they were 15 years old, boys were considered adults. They finished school and could work, marry, and vote. Girls could marry after they were 14 years old. However, not many people married this young. Even if a boy married, he had to obey his father until the father died. A girl had to obey the head of the family she married into.

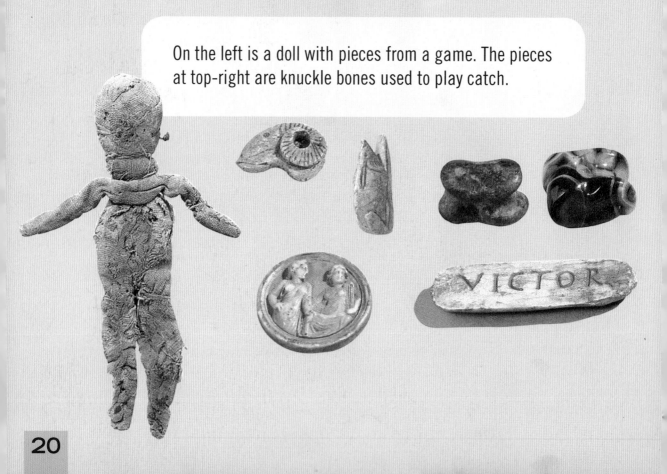

On the left is a doll with pieces from a game. The pieces at top-right are knuckle bones used to play catch.

Roman children were cared for by their mothers until they were about seven years old.

After this, boys spent most of their time with their teachers and friends.

Girls saw more of their mothers, since women were supposed to stay at home together.

Food

Romans cooked on iron stands over a fire. The fire was made on the top of a stone cooking table like this. Bread and roasted meats were cooked in brick ovens.

The Romans ate three meals a day. Breakfast was bread with honey or fruit. Lunch was bread, olives, and cheese, or food left over from the day before.

For the main meal, everyone ate bread, fruit, and vegetables. They drank wine and sweetened other foods and drinks with honey. Unlike wealthy people, poor people did not eat meat every day. Rich people ate huge main meals, especially on special occasions. Giraffes, larks, and dormice were often served, not for the flavor, but because these rare foods were status symbols.

A Wealthy Family's Kitchen

People ate mostly chicken and pork. They also hunted meat, such as this wild hare.

This slave is grinding spices. Expensive spices came from all over the **empire**.

Most people drank wine.

Romans ate lying down, propped up on their elbows. The food was served on low tables.

Entertainment

Most Romans went into towns for entertainment. They went to the theater to watch plays, listen to music, and see dancers and acrobats.

Some towns had an **arena**, which could be used for **chariot** racing. People would bet on who would win. Races were dangerous. Chariot drivers were often killed or injured.

Even more violent were the games. Wild animals were let loose in the arena to fight each other. Sometimes criminals were put into the arena to fight animals. Often they did not have weapons, or they were tied up. There was no way they could win.

This mosaic shows gladiators fighting each other in the arena.

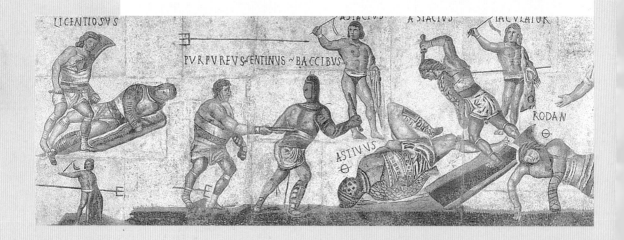

The Colosseum in Rome was the biggest Roman arena. Games held there went on for days. The arena could even be flooded for sea battles!

Trained fighters, called gladiators, fought each other. Fights were often to the death. Gladiators were criminals or slaves. Some of them fought hard and lived long enough to buy their freedom. Most died fighting.

Romans also enjoyed less violent sports. They could go to the baths, where there were places to exercise. They could race, wrestle, or play handball. Then, when they were tired, they could use the baths and go home for dinner at about 4:00 p.m.

Baths

The Romans thought it was very important to keep clean. Almost every town had public baths that anyone could use. Men and women went to separate public baths.

Wealthy people also had bath areas in their homes. These bath areas had hot, warm, and cold pools, like the public baths. This does not mean that wealthy people never went to the public baths. Romans went to the baths for more than just bathing. The baths were a place for meeting friends or doing business. There were cool, warm, and hot pools of water to swim in. There were steam rooms and places to exercise. Slaves worked at the baths, massaging people and oiling and cleaning them.

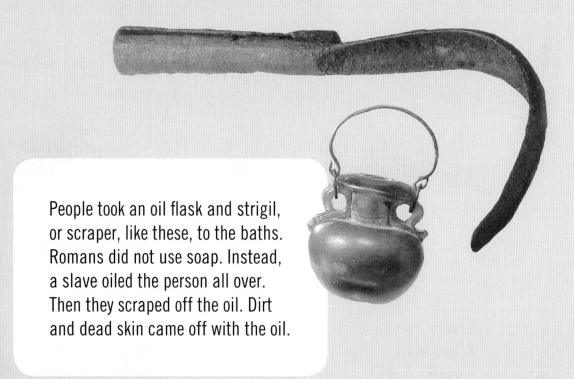

People took an oil flask and strigil, or scraper, like these, to the baths. Romans did not use soap. Instead, a slave oiled the person all over. Then they scraped off the oil. Dirt and dead skin came off with the oil.

A Public Bath House

The cold bath. People often exercised in a special area outside the baths before going to the cold room.

The hot room was hot and steamy. The water was hot, too. There was a bowl of cold water to splash in to cool down.

The next room was the warm room. In a big bath house it would have a warm pool.

People left their clothes on shelves in the changing room.

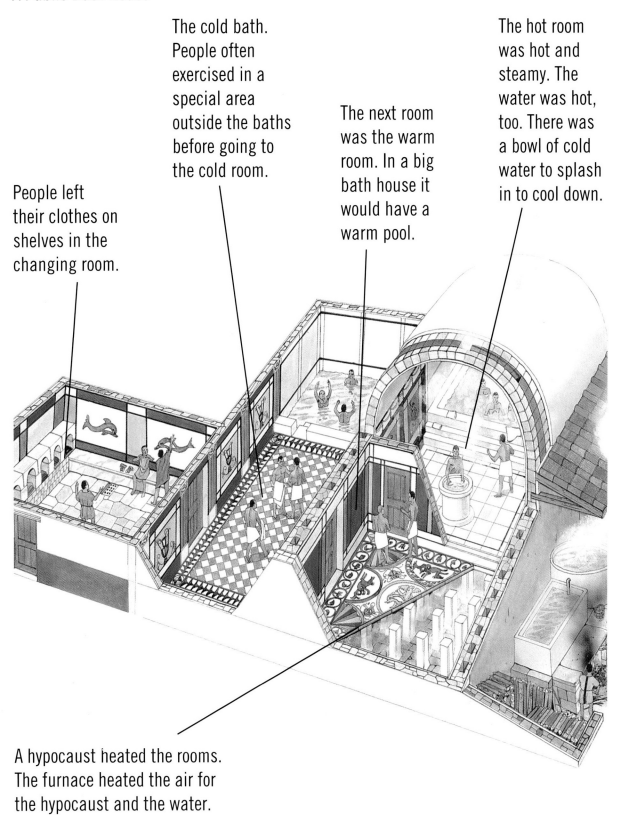

A hypocaust heated the rooms. The furnace heated the air for the hypocaust and the water.

Clothes

Most people, except the poor, wore linen underwear, usually a loose tunic. What they wore over this depended on who they were.

Men wore an outer tunic that came to about the knees. This was usually made of wool. All men except **slaves** could wear a toga, a kind of cloak folded over one shoulder and draped around the body. Women wore a long tunic that reached to the ankles. They usually wore a long cloak to go out in. Children wore similar clothes to adults.

This model of a plowman was made in Germany. People who worked outdoors in the colder provinces wore a thick, warm wool cape with a hood. It was oiled to keep out the wind and the rain.

Most clothes were made from cloth that was white, cream, or one color. Sometimes tunics had a single colored stripe around the edges or running from top to bottom. Clothes were usually washed in laundries, especially in towns.

Men wore clothes made of thick wool in winter. In summer they wore thin wool. Boots were made of leather.

Women also wore clothes made of wool. In summer, they would wear thin wool or expensive silk.

Children and slaves dressed more simply than adults. They had simpler hairstyles, too.

End of the Empire

The Roman **Empire** got too big and too difficult to govern. By AD 100 it had stopped growing. In AD 395, the empire was split into two parts, East and West. This made it easier to govern. But **barbarians** began to raid provinces on the edges of the empire. The army could not defend every province. So the Romans left some places and the empire got smaller. In AD 410, barbarians captured Rome. In AD 476 only the Eastern Empire was left. The old Roman Empire had collapsed.

Barbarians attack a town in Roman Britain. Places on the edges of the empire, as Britain was, were taken over first.

Glossary

aqueduct   bridge that carries water from one place to another

arena   flat, open place in the middle of a circular theater

barbarians   people from outside the Roman Empire

chariot   small, horse-drawn vehicle

consuls   two men who ran the Roman Republic. New ones were appointed each year.

empire   group of territories or lands controlled by one country

engineer   person who designs and builds bridges and roads

patricians   wealthy, important Roman men

plebeians   common Roman men

province   area outside Italy controlled by Rome

republic   way of running a country, using people chosen by some citizens of that country

Senate   group of wealthy and important men who ran the Roman Republic

slave   person who belongs to someone else and can be bought and sold

taxes   money you have to pay the government that runs the country

temple   place where people worship their gods or god

Find Out More

Books to read

Fix, Alexandra. *History and Activities of the Roman Empire: Hands-On Ancient History.* Chicago: Heinemann Library, 2006.

Shuter, Jane. *Life in a Roman Fort: Picture the Past.* Chicago: Heinemann Library, 2005.

Using the Internet

Explore the Internet to find out more about the ancient Romans. Use a search engine, such as www.yahooligans.com or www.internet4kids.com and type in a keyword or phrase such as "Julius Caesar" or "Colosseum."

Index